TEACH ME TO PRAY

A PRACTICAL GUIDE TO BECOME
A PERSON WHO PRAYS

TEACH ME SERIES

Elizabeth Meson

Copyright © 2015 Elizabeth Meson

All rights reserved. No part of this publication may be reproduced, stored in a retrieval system, or transmitted by any means – electronic, mechanical, photographic (photocopying), recording, or otherwise – without prior permission in writing from the author.

For more information write to:
elizabethmeson@gmail.com

Scripture taken from the HOLY BIBLE: EASY-TO-READ VERSION, ERV © 1987, 2004 by Bible League International. Used by permission.

Scripture taken from THE HOLY BIBLE, NEW INTERNATIONAL VERSION®, NIV® Copyright © 1973, 1978, 1984, 2011 by Biblica, Inc.® Used by permission. All rights reserved worldwide.

ISBN: 9798638851125

DEDICATION

To my mother, who for as long as I can remember has been a person who prays daily, consistently, and for a huge list of people. You are my hero! And to all those new and old believers who struggle to pray daily; you are my inspiration!

CONTENT

INTRODUCTION	1
GET STARTED	3
WORSHIP	5
GIVE THANKS	8
ASK FOR FORGIVENESS	11
EXPRESS NEEDS	14
MAKE REQUESTS	17
SURRENDER	20
SHARE SPIRITUAL STRUGGLES	23
WRAP UP	26
CONCLUSION	29
ABOUT THE AUTHOR	30

INTRODUCTION

I have had a prayer relationship with God since I was a child. My parents always prayed and gave us ample opportunities to pray. But as the years went by, I realized I wanted prayer to be more personal and real to me. When I was going through spiritual revival it was easy to pray, when I was struggling with problems, I was quick to cry out to God. But during the rest of my life, I found that it was hard to pray consistently and in a significant way. Either my mind couldn't focus, or things around me caught my attention and I'd quickly forget I was praying. On many days I wouldn't even remember God was waiting to meet with me!

It was then I decided that to become a person who prayed consistently I needed to do that which I did every day to be productive. I made lists for the things I needed to get done; so, I thought a list for prayer was a great idea. I also realized I needed to make that list more proactive and practical, so I developed the parts of prayer with the starting words and ideas that could be completed by filling in the blanks with my own words. And it began to work! I found I was focusing on my prayers and thinking about what I was praying. My mind didn't wander, because the initial thought was written down in front of me.

Sometimes I would choose only a few items to pray because I only had a few minutes; but those few moments were more profitable than the longer periods of prayer of the past. Other days I would take my time to slowly go through each item and develop the thought before God, and it was extremely beneficial and rewarding.

In the same way it helps us to follow step-by-step instructions to exercise, make a dessert, take medication or follow treatment the doctor prescribes, it also helps us to have specific steps to become persons of prayer.

I can't tell you exactly what and how to talk to someone, but when the conversation gets awkward, I can help you get started. Many people have a relationship with God, but when it comes to communication, they feel awkward talking to him. With this booklet I hope to help you start the conversation, so it flows from there. God wants you to express yourself to him in every area of your life. When your mind goes blank and you don't know what to say, I hope to help you start that process flowing. Finally, you will find that talking to God daily will become your most needed and satisfying experience. Take the leap of faith and try it, you won't be disappointed!

GET STARTED

Hebrews 10:19-23 – Therefore, brothers and sisters, since we have confidence to enter the Most Holy Place by the blood of Jesus, by a new and living way opened for us through the curtain, that is, his body, and since we have a great priest over the house of God, let us draw near to God with a sincere heart and with the full assurance that faith brings, having our hearts sprinkled to cleanse us from a guilty conscience and having our bodies washed with pure water. Let us hold unswervingly to the hope we profess, for he who promised is faithful. (NIV)

Everyone has a better time of day to pray; but it's a certainty that we need prayer at all times. Our conversations with others are spontaneous and happen at any time throughout our day or night. That's how it should be with God.

The truth is that we have to be able and ready at any moment to talk to God and allow him to talk to us. This tool can go with you on your phone or on your tablet, or you can have a printed version in your purse or your backpack. You could be riding in a car, the bus, or subway, or waiting for an appointment and be able to pull it out and use it in any order you prefer.

You can also carve out a specific time in your day to have a good deep talk with God. That is so important so you're not just a fire fighter in your prayer life. What I mean, is that you don't want prayer to be used only in emergencies; prayer should be a loving relationship with God on a spontaneous and daily basis.

Each chapter title tells you what to do. You can start with any chapter and move along as you wish. Each day you can choose where you want to begin and from there follow in any order as you are led to pray. I have added verses at the beginning of each chapter that will help you understand what God has to say to you about each specific kind of prayer. You can read one or all as a way of listening to what God has to say to you and where he gets the conversation going. In your digital version you can hold and press next to a word or phrase and it will allow you to write a comment or highlight it. In the hard copy version, I have provided space for you to write your comments.

I hope you will be as blessed as I am to have those flowing conversations with God; and be assured that he hears you and wants you to share everything that's in your heart with Him.

Hebrews 12:1-3 – Therefore, since we are surrounded by such a great cloud of witnesses, let us throw off everything that hinders and the sin that so easily entangles. And let us run with perseverance the race marked out for us, fixing our eyes on Jesus, the pioneer and perfecter of faith. For the joy set before him he endured the cross, scorning its shame, and sat down at the right hand of the throne of God. Consider him who endured such opposition from sinners, so that you will not grow weary and lose heart. (NIV)

WORSHIP

God says:

John 4:23-24 – But the time is coming when the true worshipers will worship the Father in spirit and truth. In fact, that time is now here. And these are the kind of people the Father wants to be his worshipers. God is spirit. So the people who worship him must worship in spirit and truth. (ERV)

Romans 12:1 – Therefore, I urge you, brothers and sisters, in view of God's mercy, to offer your bodies as a living sacrifice, holy and pleasing to God—this is your true and proper worship. (NIV)

Psalm 150: 1-6 – Praise the Lord. Praise God in his sanctuary; praise him in his mighty heavens. Praise him for his acts of power; praise him for his surpassing greatness. Praise him with the sounding of the trumpet, praise him with the harp and lyre, praise him with timbrel and dancing, praise him with the strings and pipe, praise him with the clash of cymbals, praise him with resounding cymbals. Let everything that has breath praise the Lord. Praise the Lord. (NIV)

Hebrews 13:15 – Through Jesus, therefore, let us continually offer to God a sacrifice of praise—the fruit of lips that openly profess his name. (NIV)

You say:

When you love someone, you praise them and give them your affection, your loyalty and admiration. That is what worship is and much much more.

When you worship God, you honor and give him your devotion. You exalt him and praise him for who he is and what he does.

Who is God to you?

Lord, you are…

- -my shepherd.
- -my Father.
- -the love of my life.
- -my fortress.
- -my light.
- -the beginning and the end.

Lord, I acknowledge…

- -your greatness.
- -your sovereignty.
- -your guidance in my life.
- -you have control over all

I give you praise for…

- -loving me.
- -helping me.
- -leading me.
- -for defending me.
- -for being so great and powerful.
- -your loving kindness.

TEACH ME TO PRAY

GIVE THANKS

God says:
1 Thessalonians 5:18 –...give thanks in all circumstances; for this is God's will for you in Christ Jesus. (NIV)

Psalm 100:1-5 – Earth, sing to the Lord! Be happy as you serve the Lord! Come before him with happy songs! Know that the Lord is God. He made us, and we belong to him. We are his people, the sheep he takes care of. Come through the gates to his Temple giving thanks to him. Enter his courtyards with songs of praise. Honor him and bless his name. The Lord is good! There is no end to his faithful love. We can trust him forever and ever! (ERV)

Philippians 4:6 – Do not be anxious about anything, but in every situation, by prayer and petition, with thanksgiving, present your requests to God. (NIV)

Psalm 118:21 – Lord, I thank you for answering my prayer. I thank you for saving me. (ERV)

1 Chronicles 29:12-13 – Wealth and honor come from you; you are the ruler of all things. In your hands are strength and power to exalt and give strength to all. Now, our God, we give you thanks, and praise your glorious name. (NIV)

You say:
Thankfulness is acknowledging what a person did and showing gratitude towards them. We respond with

appreciation for the grace and consideration shown us. Being thankful is recognizing that God wants the best for us and loves us with an eternal and deep love.

What are you thankful for?

Thank you that...

   -you are with me.

   -you provide for me.

   -you give me wisdom.

   -you protect me.

   -you help me with _____.

Thank you for...

   -guarding my family from evil.

   -providing for them.

   -deliverance and healing.

   -helping me _____.

I'm grateful to you for...

   -helping me in my daily activities.

   -saving me.

   -giving me your Spirit.

   -teaching me your Word.

   -giving me peace.

   -helping me in _____ situation.

   -my job.

   -my school.

   -my family.

ELIZABETH MESON

ASK FOR FORGIVENESS

God says:
1 John 1:9 – But if we confess our sins, God will forgive us. We can trust God to do this. He always does what is right. He will make us clean from all the wrong things we have done. (ERV)

Psalm 103:10-14 – We sinned against him, but he didn't give us the punishment we deserved. His love for his followers is as high above us as heaven is above the earth. And he has taken our sins as far away from us as the east is from the west. The Lord is as kind to his followers as a father is to his children. He knows all about us. He knows we are made from dust. (ERV)

Micah 7:18-19 – There is no God like you. You take away people's guilt. God will forgive his people who survive. He will not stay angry with them forever, because he enjoys being kind. He will come back and comfort us again. He will throw all our sins into the deep sea. (ERV)

Acts 10:43 – All the prophets testify about him that everyone who believes in him receives forgiveness of sins through his name. (NIV)

Psalm 32:5 – But then I decided to confess my sins to the Lord. I stopped hiding my guilt and told you about my sins. And you forgave them all! (ERV)

You say
When we've done wrong, we need to make it right.

Forgiveness is a crucial part of our Christian life; it is the basis of our salvation. Without forgiveness we can't move on and grow as children of God. When we ask for forgiveness, we admit that we are wrong and humble ourselves before God to receive his mercy and grace.

What are you sorry for?

I ask you Lord to forgive me for…

   -not trusting you.

   -putting you in second place.

   -not reading your Word.

Forgive me for the sin of…

_____.

Cleanse me with your blood for…

   -lying.

   -deceiving.

   -holding a grudge.

   -gossiping.

   -putting _____ down.

I confess I struggle with…

   -anger.

   -addiction.

   -hating myself.

   -lack of forgiveness.

   -doubt.

TEACH ME TO PRAY

EXPRESS NEEDS

God says:
Philippians 4:6 – Don't worry about anything, but pray and ask God for everything you need, always giving thanks for what you have. (ERV)

Philippians 4:19 – And my God will meet all your needs according to the riches of his glory in Christ Jesus. (NIV)

Matthew 6:31-32 – Don't worry and say, 'What will we eat?' or 'What will we drink?' or 'What will we wear?' That's what those people who don't know God are always thinking about. Don't worry, because your Father in heaven knows that you need all these things. (ERV)

Psalm 34:10 – Even strong lions get weak and hungry, but those who go to the Lord for help will have every good thing. (ERV)

John 14:26 – But the Advocate, the Holy Spirit, whom the Father will send in my name, will teach you all things and will remind you of everything I have said to you. (NIV)

2 Corinthians 9:8 – And God is able to bless you abundantly, so that in all things at all times, having all that you need, you will abound in every good work. (NIV)

You say:
God wants us to express our needs to him. He cares for us and wants to supply our needs. We feel vulnerable

when we have a need and sometimes want to hide the fact. But God is our father and friend and wants us to trust him enough to express ourselves like children that don't hold anything back. As you practice putting your needs before God, he will teach you how to ask and what to ask for as he grows and leads you into maturity.

What is your need?

Lord, I need…

- -you to speak to me from your Word.
- -a better way to manage my finances.
- -help at work, school, home.
- -you to fill my loneliness.
- -to learn to pray.

Father I lack…

- -faith.
- -understanding.
- -a forgiving heart.
- -patience.
- -healing.

I bring to you…

- -my heavy heart.
- -my workload.
- -my difficult studies.
- -my relationship with my spouse.
- -my relationship with my children.

ELIZABETH MESON

MAKE REQUESTS

God says:
Matthew 7:7 – Continue to ask, and God will give to you. Continue to search, and you will find. Continue to knock, and the door will open for you. (ERV)

John 15:7 – If you remain in me and my words remain in you, ask whatever you wish, and it will be done for you. (NIV)

1 John 5:14 – This is the confidence we have in approaching God: that if we ask anything according to his will, he hears us. (NIV)

Matthew 21:22 – If you believe, you will get anything you ask for in prayer. (ERV)

James 4:3 – Or when you ask, you don't receive anything, because the reason you ask is wrong. You only want to use it for your own pleasure. (ERV)

James 1:6-8 – But when you ask, you must believe and not doubt, because the one who doubts is like a wave of the sea, blown and tossed by the wind. That person should not expect to receive anything from the Lord. Such a person is double-minded and unstable in all they do. (NIV)

James 5:14-15 – Are you sick? Ask the elders of the church to come and rub oil on you in the name of the Lord and pray for you. If such a prayer is offered in faith, it will heal anyone who is sick. The Lord will heal them. And if they have sinned, he will forgive them. (ERV)

You say:

Making a request is different from expressing needs. When you ask for something, you are standing in the gap to make a request for yourself or for someone else, or to intercede in prayer for yourself or for someone else. A request is a desire or a need to attain something. God wants to give us his riches in glory! And we need to have faith! Something else to ask for.

What do you want to ask for?

Lord, I pray for...

- -my neighbor's salvation.
- -provision for rent, bills, _____.
- -healing for _____.
- -understanding of your Word.
- -my community to know you.

Lord, I ask you...

- -for the spiritual gift of _____.
- -to provide _____.
- -for a word to share with _____.
- -intelligence to face _____.
- -for _____.
- -wisdom and guidance.

TEACH ME TO PRAY

SURRENDER

God says:
2 Chronicles 7:14 – …and if my people who are called by my name become humble and pray, and look for me, and turn away from their evil ways, then I will hear them from heaven. I will forgive their sin and heal their land. (ERV)

James 4:7 – Submit yourselves, then, to God. Resist the devil, and he will flee from you. (NIV)

Romans 12:2 – Do not conform to the pattern of this world, but be transformed by the renewing of your mind. Then you will be able to test and approve what God's will is—his good, pleasing and perfect will. (NIV)

John 15:4-5 – Remain in me, as I also remain in you. No branch can bear fruit by itself; it must remain in the vine. Neither can you bear fruit unless you remain in me. (NIV)

Proverbs 23:26 – My son, give me your heart and let your eyes delight in my way. (NIV)

Matthew 11:28 – Come to me, all you who are weary and burdened, and I will give you rest. (NIV)

You say:
The word surrender means to relinquish a hold on something, to yield as you would at a traffic stop. You give way to someone else; and that someone is God. He wants you to be willing to give him the chance to work in you

and through you. This part of prayer is where you give up to God those areas or things that you know have taken his place.

What do you want to let go of?

Lord, I surrender…

   -my problem of _____.

   -wanting to resolve _____.

   -the busyness of my life.

   -the activity of: _____.

   -and put _____in your hands.

Jesus, I give you…

   -my heart.

   -my life.

   -my dreams.

   -my goals.

I want you to have control over…

   -my family.

   -my decisions.

   -my work.

   -my studies.

   -my home.

   -this problem of _____.

ELIZABETH MESON

SHARE SPIRITUAL STRUGGLES

God says:
Ephesians 6:12 – Our fight is not against people on earth. We are fighting against the rulers and authorities and the powers of this world's darkness. We are fighting against the spiritual powers of evil in the heavenly places. (ERV).

2 Timothy 1:7 – The Spirit God gave us does not make us afraid. His Spirit is a source of power and love and self-control. (ERV)

Ephesians 6:11 – Put on the full armor of God, so that you can take your stand against the devil's schemes. (ERV)

2 Corinthians 10:3-5 – For though we live in the world, we do not wage war as the world does. The weapons we fight with are not the weapons of the world. On the contrary, they have divine power to demolish strongholds. We demolish arguments and every pretension that sets itself up against the knowledge of God, and we take captive every thought to make it obedient to Christ. (NIV)

Deuteronomy 28:7 – The Lord will grant that the enemies who rise up against you will be defeated before you. They will come at you from one direction but flee from you in seven. (NIV)

James 4:7 – So give yourselves to God. Stand against the devil, and he will run away from you. (ERV)

You say:
We all have a battle going on with the powers of evil.

Jesus said he overcame the world and defeated Satan. We need God's power to guard us, and faith to trust that he is able to deliver us.

What are you struggling with?

Lord, help me to…

- -pray.
- -have faith.
- -forgive.
- -read the Bible.
- -trust you.
- -be faithful to you.
- -put on your armor.

In the name of Jesus, I submit to you…

- -my thoughts.
- -my faith.
- -my talents and spiritual gifts.
- -my family.
- -my church.

Lord, with your blood cover and guard from Satan's oppression…

- -my home.
- -my conversation.
- -my emotions.
- -my health.

TEACH ME TO PRAY

WRAP UP

God says:

Colossians 3:17 – And whatever you do, whether in word or deed, do it all in the name of the Lord Jesus, giving thanks to God the Father through him. (NIV)

Psalm 8:1 – Lord, our Lord, how majestic is your name in all the earth! You have set your glory in the heavens. (NIV)

Psalm 148:13 – Praise the Lord's name! Honor his name forever! His name is greater than any other. He is more glorious than heaven and earth. (ERV)

John 14:13 – And if you ask for anything in my name, I will do it for you. Then the Father's glory will be shown through the Son. (ERV)

John 15:16 – You did not choose me, but I chose you and appointed you so that you might go and bear fruit—fruit that will last—and so that whatever you ask in my name the Father will give you. (NIV)

Jeremiah 33:3 – Call to me and I will answer you and tell you great and unsearchable things you do not know. (NIV)

Proverbs 18:10 – The name of the Lord is like a strong tower. Those who do what is right can run to him for protection. (ERV)

You say:

We end our prayer in the name of Jesus. We pray to the Father through Jesus his son. He is interceding for us in the presence of God. We join him in his intercession when we pray to him. Remember to give him the glory and honor he deserves when you talk to him.

In whose name will you pray?

Jesus in your name I...

    -offer you everything I say and do.

    -ask for your blessing upon my life.

    -bring all my petitions before you.

    -ask that you preserve my words.

In the powerful name of Jesus, I...

    -acknowledge you as my Savior.

    -place in you my home and family.

    -declare peace upon my life.

    -rise up victorious.

    -take captive all thoughts to you.

    - surrender my heart completely to you.

Amen, let your will be done in my life Lord Jesus, my Savior, and my God.

ELIZABETH MESON

CONCLUSION

My hope is that this small booklet will help you start a prayer relationship with God. I'm eager to show you how wonderful it is to spend time in prayer and the satisfaction, peace, and positive outcome that praying produces, becoming your motivation to continue to pray.

The Lord Jesus gave his disciples a model to help them pray. That is exactly what this booklet does; it's a template for prayer. The concept is simple; God speaks through his word first and then you use the list to get your conversation with God going and keep you focused on your prayers. This tool will help you pray for five, ten, twenty, or more minutes depending on the time you have to dedicate to it. Where there are blanks, fill them in as you feel led or with the particular situation that comes to mind, then present that to God.

Start wherever you want to; there is no specific order to prayer like any other conversation you could have with a friend. Pray some items, pray all the items listed; what is more, just follow what your heart dictates or your mind directs, and the Holy Spirit will take it from there.

Finally, I know from experience from several years of using this tool that it is worthwhile to have. God will teach you to pray and you can truthfully say that you have become a person who prays. God bless you in this endeavor!

ABOUT THE AUTHOR

Elizabeth Meson was born to missionary parents and raised in Argentina. She grew up in a home where it was normal and encouraged to have a relationship with God. She married a man who is passionate about serving God, and after a few years of managing their businesses, they sold them and went into full-time ministry. They have served and planted a number of churches in Argentina, and in 2001, she and her husband came to the United States after sensing God's call on their lives to plant churches among the Hispanic people of Central Pennsylvania.

She has been in ministry for many years and is very familiar and passionate about helping people grow in their walk with God; hence her eagerness to share practical ways to grow in that personal day-to-day walk with God and build good healthy habits that help make Christianity a reality.

Elizabeth is the mother of five children and grandmother of eleven grandchildren and counting.

Made in United States
Orlando, FL
17 March 2024